Governor Zell Miller's
Reading Initiative

JULIUS CAESAR

JULIUS CAESAR

BY
ROBERT GREEN

A FIRST BOOK

FRANKLIN WATTS
A DIVISION OF GROLIER PUBLISHING
NEW YORK – LONDON – HONG KONG – SYDNEY
DANBURY, CONNECTICUT

For D.R. Green

Cover design by Robin Hoffmann

Map by MacArt Design

Photo credits ©: AKG Photo: p. 18 (Jutus Göpel); Art Resource: pp. 8, 34 (both photos Giraudon), 10, 11, 12, 15, 30 (all photos Scala); Bettmann Archive: cover, pp. 2, 24, 37; Bridgeman Art Library: p. 38 (Giraudon); Hulton Deutsch Collection: p. 22; Mary Evans Picture Libary: pp. 20, 43, 48, 55; North Wind Picture Archives: pp. 36, 46; The Orchard: p. 41 (C. M. Dixon); Stock Montage, Inc.: p. 57; Superstock, Inc.: pp. 28, 51.

Consultant: Allen M. Ward, University of Connecticut.

Library of Congress Cataloging-in-Publication Data

Green, Robert.
Julius Caesar / by Robert Green.
p. cm. — (A First Book)
Includes bibliographical references and index.
Summary: A biography of the Roman general and statesman whose brilliant military leadership helped make Rome the center of a vast empire.
ISBN 0-531-20241-0 (lib. bdg.) — ISBN 0-531-15812-8 (pbk.)
1. Caesar, Julius—Juvenile literature. 2. Heads of state—Rome—Biography—Juvenile literature. 3. Generals—Rome—Biography—Juvenile literature.
4. Rome—History—Republic, 265–30 B.C.—Juvenile literature. [1. Caesar, Julius. 2. Heads of state. 3. Generals. 4. Rome—History—Republic, 265–30 B.C.] I. Title. II. Series.
DG261.G69 1996
937'.05'092—dc20   *96-7277 CIP AC*
[B]

CONTENTS

That civilisation may not sink
Its great battle lost,
Quiet the dog, tether the pony
To a distant post.
Our master Caesar is in the tent
Where the maps are spread,
His eyes fixed upon nothing,
A hand under his head.
Like a long-legged fly upon the stream
His mind moves upon silence.

—WILLIAM BUTLER YEATS,
FROM *LONG-LEGGED FLY*

1

CAESAR AND ROME

On March 15, 44 B.C. (the Ides of March), Julius Caesar was to meet with the Roman Senate. He didn't want to go. He did not feel well, and his wife had terrible dreams that he was in danger. One of the senators, Marcus Junius Brutus, went to Caesar's house and persuaded him to go to the meeting.

Caesar had just been named dictator for life. As he was escorted in a procession through the city, the curious citizens crowded the streets to see their leader pass by. Caesar had been very good to the common people, so most Romans supported him. But many did not like being ruled by a dictator. Some senators were very upset, because having a dictator would greatly reduce their powers.

Caesar departs for the Senate on the Ides of March, 44 B.C., as his wife Calpurnia faints. She had dreamed the night before that Caesar was in great danger.

As Caesar made his way to the Senate, someone pressed a message into his hand, but he ignored it. When he entered the Senate building and took his seat, the senators slowly moved toward him. They spoke calmly as they circled him.

Suddenly they struck. One after another, they plunged their daggers into his body. When he realized he could not flee, he used his toga to try to fend off the strikes. But they stabbed him twenty-three times, and his toga only soaked up his blood.

In Caesar's hand, they found the crumpled message he had received on his way in. It warned him of the conspiracy against him. He hadn't even read it. The most powerful man in Rome had been assassinated by a group of Roman aristocrats.

How did Caesar take control of Rome, and why was he killed at the height of his power? He won power with brilliant military and political tactics. He had great influence over his troops and over many people. But in his rise to power, Caesar had made many enemies. His assassins, some of whom were his friends, killed him to try to save the old government. It was too late. Caesar had changed the way Rome was ruled. After his death, Rome was plunged into years of civil war, and eventually the senators were forced to give way to an emperor. For hundreds of years, the Roman Empire would control much of the Mediterranean world.

Caesar is helpless to defend himself as the conspirators in the Senate plunge their daggers repeatedly into his body. He falls at the foot of a statue of his old enemy Pompey.

ROMAN GOVERNMENT

According to legend, Rome was founded in 753 B.C. At first it was just a tiny kingdom—one city and a little land. Over hundreds of years Romans waged war and forged alliances to gain control of most of the Italian peninsula.

Romulus and Remus, the mythical founders of Rome, are suckled by the she-wolf. It was at the Lupercalia, the festival of the she-wolf, that Marc Antony tried to crown Caesar the king of Rome. Caesar resisted the honor so as not to offend the Roman Senate.

The kingdom became a republic, governed by an unwritten constitution based on customs and laws. This government was dominated by aristocrats, men who owned land and slaves. Only men who held important public positions could become senators. All free men could vote for officials or new laws, but only the elected officials—the aristocrats—could present laws for a vote.

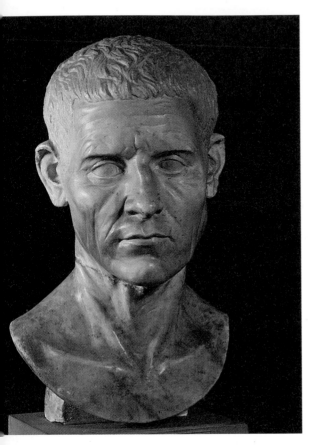

Lucius Cornelius Sulla

The highest government officials were the *consuls*. Romans elected two consuls each year, who shared civic and military responsibilities. This way, no one man could become a tyrant and seize Rome's power and wealth. If a serious crisis came up, like war or famine, they would elect one man dictator, but only for a six-month term.

The two-consul system prevented a takeover by one man, but it allowed a small group of aristocrats to control power. The men who already served as consuls would try to get other members of their families elected next. Many senators became corrupt as they competed for these positions.

When Caesar was born, in 100 B.C., the Roman Republic was the greatest power in the land around the Mediterranean. Under Lucius Cornelius Sulla, the army and navy expanded Roman influence west as far as Spain, east into ancient Syria, and south into Africa. These lands ruled by Rome were called provinces. Each province was ruled by a governor. All Roman provinces paid a tax, called tribute, to Rome. They paid in gold, silver, trade goods, or even food. Rome became a very rich city.

POPULARES AND OPTIMATES

As Rome gained power, the competition to become a consul became more intense. Some politicians won elections by promising to help the poor. There were no political parties in ancient Rome, so powerful families made alliances with each other that constantly changed.

The aristocrats who appealed to the poorest people came from families that did not control the consulship at the time. They were called *populares*. The families that did influence the consuls called themselves *optimates* ("the good men"). They feared they would lose power if discontented people were attracted to outsiders. They also worried that an outsider might draw popular support and become a tyrant. Both sides hired gangs of street thugs to influence people's opinions. Violence became a part of Roman politics, and a politician who failed in office could be killed.

In 88 B.C., a great struggle broke out when a populare named Gaius Marius and his allies fought against the optimate Sulla and his supporters. Sulla won. He captured Rome in 82 B.C. after a series of civil wars. He was elected dictator, but no term limit was given. Marius had died during the fighting, and during Caesar's youth Sulla ruthlessly attacked Marius's old allies.

CAESAR'S FAMILY

Caesar grew up in a busy neighborhood near the Forum, the center of Roman public life. He was ambitious from an early age. His parents nominated him to become a priest of Jupiter in 87 B.C. Jupiter was the most powerful of all the Roman gods. Caesar's family was quite religious, but that wasn't why they wanted him to get the priesthood. Becoming a priest would give him access to powerful politicians.

Caesar's family were patricians, members of Rome's old aristocracy. The Julii, as they were called, claimed they could trace their roots to the goddess

Jupiter was the principal god of the Romans. The Priesthood of Jupiter was a prestigious office, one that provided Caesar with introductions to many important Romans.

Venus. By Caesar's time, though, patrician families were no longer very powerful. His father, Gaius Caesar, died when Caesar was sixteen years old.

When Caesar was young, two of his relatives were consuls. But his family was mostly on the side of the populares. Marius had even been married to Caesar's aunt Julia. Because of his family and the connection to Marius, Caesar sided with the populares rather than with Sulla and the optimates.

To further advance his early career, Caesar married Cornelia, the daughter of Cornelius Cinna, in 84 B.C. Cinna was Marius's closest ally and became a leader of the populares. Sulla still opposed the populares and wanted to separate Caesar from them, so he ordered Caesar to divorce Cornelia. Caesar refused and was forced into exile to escape Sulla's wrath. In 80 B.C. he sailed east, where he served the Roman governor of Asia. He became friends with King Nicomedes IV of Bithynia, a small country on the Black Sea. Nicomedes was impressed with Caesar and showed him firsthand how Bithynia was run.

After Sulla died, in 78 B.C., Caesar returned to Rome to try out his skills as an orator (public speaker) in the law courts. It's been said that Caesar could have surpassed Cicero, the greatest orator of Rome, for he was a talented speaker and writer. But Caesar's future would take him in a different direction— toward the very peak of power in the Roman world.

2

THE LEAGUE OF THREE

When Julius Caesar was twenty-five, he set sail for the island of Rhodes to study oratory. But on the way, a band of pirates captured the ship and kidnapped him. While his family was raising ransom money, Caesar was a very difficult "guest" of the pirates. He strolled boldly around their ship, pointed out weaknesses in their swordfighting technique, and told them he would kill them all after he was released! They were entertained by him but did not believe the threat.

Then, Caesar's ransom was paid and the pirates released him. He then learned, however, that the Roman governor was not interested in pursuing the pirates. Caesar took the law into his own hands. He

Caesar was known among Romans as a pleasure-seeker. When he saw a statue of Alexander the Great in Spain, though, he knew that he had to make a name for himself as a military commander.

organized a fleet of ships, captured the pirates, and crucified the entire gang. News of his actions spread quickly. He was both admired and criticized for acting so swiftly and independently.

By age thirty, Caesar was making Sulla's allies very worried. But thirty was not young for a Roman so full of ambition. In 69 B.C. Caesar was serving as governor in Farther Spain, administering Roman justice to Spanish tribes and subduing those that resisted. In the city of Cadiz, Caesar went to see a statue of Alexander the Great (356–323 B.C.), the famous king of Macedonia who had conquered much of the world by age thirty. Caesar, remembering that, wept out of envy. He was far from Rome and wanted to get back into politics and make his mark.

POMPEY AND CRASSUS

Caesar admired and studied the two most successful Romans of his day, Pompey and Crassus. He followed their ways in shaping his own career. The two men were very different. Pompey rose to power through military victories in North Africa, Spain, and the East, while Crassus used financial savvy to influence politicians and become the richest man in Rome. It was said that Crassus bought valuable property in Rome by making offers on the spot for burning buildings and the threatened buildings nearby.

By 67 B.C., Caesar was back in Rome. His wife, Cornelia, had died two years before. He took a new wife, Pompeia, and used her money to enter politics. He also became friends with Pompey. A debate raged in the Senate over the pirates in the Mediterranean who terrorized the Roman shipping lanes. Pompey had been consul in 70 B.C., but he wanted instead to lead the Roman fleet in defending against the pirates of the Mediterranean.

Caesar helped Pompey get command of a fleet. Pompey set sail and did not return to Rome until 62 B.C. Meanwhile, Caesar became friends with Crassus, who liked to guide promising young men through the twists and turns of Roman political life. Caesar was a favorite with Marius's old followers, and Crassus thought Caesar would be a perfect student.

CAESAR ENTERS POLITICS

Caesar loved to spend money and was constantly in debt. Roman politics was an expensive business. Crassus and others advanced Caesar enormous loans. Soon Caesar was elected to the post of *curule aedile*—caretaker of Rome's buildings, streets, and public sanitation—for the year 65 B.C. The curule aedile also entertained the Romans by staging public games. During the games, gladiators, who were slaves and criminals, fought to the death with swords, and charioteers raced madly around oval tracks.

Caesar had the best games Rome had ever seen. He spent huge sums of borrowed money. He even decorated gladiators' armor with silver during special games, in memory of his father. He was becoming a celebrity in Rome.

Roman life revolved around the happenings at the Forum, where many statues and temples celebrated Rome's gods and great citizens. Caesar used some of the spoils of the Gallic Wars to construct a marble temple dedicated to Venus Genetrix, a goddess from whom it was believed Caesar's family was descended.

Caesar pleased the Roman public by providing lavish gladiatorial games when he served as curule aedile *in Rome. Here a gladiator looks to a group of aristocratic spectators to determine the fate of his wounded opponent. They are giving him a "thumbs down" sign, meaning he should spare the wounded man's life; thumbs up would have meant they wanted to see the man's death.*

Two years later Caesar bribed the right people in order to win election as *pontifex maximus* (high priest), a position of great political importance. The official residence of the pontifex maximus was the Regia, a special house in the Forum. With this title, Caesar could grant favors to his friends and creditors. In fact, on the day of the election he told his mother not to expect him home if he lost, because his creditors would demand payment in blood.

Caesar was elected *praetor* (high-ranking judge) in 62 B.C. but soon suffered a major embarrassment. An ambitious young aristocrat named Publius Clodius disguised himself as a woman and entered a sacred religious festival of the Good Goddess, a deity worshiped only by women. Some people thought that Clodius was planning to seduce Caesar's wife, Pompeia. Caesar wanted to divorce her anyway, because she had not given birth to a child. So he used the scandal with Clodius as his excuse. Pompeia asked Caesar why she, the innocent victim, was the one to be punished. He answered, "Caesar's wife must be above suspicion."

Caesar was chosen to go to Farther Spain again, this time as *proconsul* (governor of a Roman province who acted in place of a consul). He took this opportunity to collect much-needed money from rich silver mines and from conquered tribes. Some of the tribes rebelled. The Romans, under Caesar's command,

The Roman footsoldier, or legionnaire, was the foundation of Rome's professional army. Legionnaires were rigorously trained and outfitted with useful equipment: javelin, sword, shield, and light armor.

beat them back with their feared short swords and iron-tipped javelins.

While Caesar governed Farther Spain, Pompey defeated the pirates who attacked Roman ships in the Mediterranean. He also won a major victory in Asia Minor (modern Turkey) over Mithradates, a longtime enemy of Rome. Pompey now was so popular with Romans that the optimates feared he might return with his army and declare himself dictator. To their surprise, he laid down his arms when he arrived. He was welcomed as a hero, but his enemies in the Senate blocked attempts to reward his soldiers for their victories.

Caesar sensed that the moment was right for bringing Pompey and Crassus, who were rivals, into a coalition with him. They formed the First Triumvirate, or league of three, in 60 B.C. All three disagreed with the optimate senators, and their unofficial alliance took a lot of power from the Senate.

To seal the alliance, Pompey married Caesar's daughter, Julia. She had been born around 76 B.C. to Caesar's first wife, Cornelia. Pompey and Crassus backed Caesar for the consulship for 59 B.C., and Caesar won. He now held the highest office in the government of Rome. He overpowered the other consul, Bibulus, an ally of the optimates. He also married a third time, to Calpurnia, whose father became a consul in 58 B.C. Then Caesar had certain laws passed that would benefit Pompey and Crassus.

Cato the Younger, one of the most respected optimate leaders, opposed the Triumvirate. In order to keep him from stirring up trouble in Rome, the three leaders sent Cato away as governor of the island of Cyprus. The optimates, now alarmed by the shift of power, were also terrorized by street gangs.

The Triumvirate was an uneasy alliance. All three men were ambitious; Crassus and Pompey each wanted sole control of Rome. Caesar's goal was to become greater than either of them. In order to reach that goal, he knew he needed huge amounts of money, military glory, and the allegiance of a strong army.

When Caesar's consulship ended in 59 B.C., he was awarded the position of proconsul in Gaul. With this office he would recruit and train an army that would be loyal to him. He then set out on what would become one of the bloodiest military campaigns in history.

3
THE GALLIC WARS

Gaul to the Romans meant three areas: Cisalpine Gaul, near the Alps mountain range in Italy; Transalpine Gaul, in southern France; and independent Gaul, stretching to the Atlantic Ocean in the west and north and to the Rhine River in the east. It was still a wild land, and the Romans had been harassed by tribes crossing the Alps and entering Italy to escape from Germanic invaders. Caesar set out to conquer Gaul, starting with the Helvetii, a tribe in what is now Switzerland.

Caesar was middle-aged in 58 B.C. when he marched north. He was used to a good lifestyle in Rome. But he also proved to be as tough as the toughest soldiers, enduring the same hardships, willing to

Before setting out for Gaul, Caesar put on a blood-red cloak and the civic crown. He is supposed to have favored this crown above all other honors because it covered his bald spots.

sleep on the cold ground or to lead a battle. His pride set a wonderful example for his soldiers, and they became very devoted to him. He soon showed them he was a military genius, too.

ON THE BATTLEFIELD

After Caesar crossed the Alps, he received news that the Helvetii were fleeing into Gaul. Caesar confronted them and ordered them to return to Switzerland. They refused. The Helvetii outnumbered the Romans, so Caesar waited for reinforcements from Cisalpine Gaul, then attacked.

The Roman soldiers were talented fighters who kept close to one another and marched forward in well-ordered lines. They slaughtered the Helvetii and hunted down those who fled the body-strewn battlefield. Even women and children were not spared from massacre. The few who escaped death were forced back to Switzerland.

Caesar then turned to the growing number of Germans in the area led by Ariovistus. Like other German fighters, Ariovistus had long braids and wore decorative silver and gold armbands. He refused to meet Caesar for negotiations and rejected written demands to leave.

The Roman troops were frightened by stories of how fiercely the Germans fought, but Caesar raised

This striking figure, called the Dying Gaul, *represents the pain of the Gallic warriors' losses to the Romans.*

their morale with a brilliant speech. He was full of confidence as he described his military plan. When the two armies approached each other again, Ariovistus agreed to a personal meeting with Caesar.

Ariovistus demanded that the Romans retreat. Caesar, draped in his blood-red cloak, listened to Ariovistus quietly. He must have been amused by the stubbornness of Ariovistus, because Caesar was never afraid to fight. He refused to compromise. The two armies met near the Rhine River, where France borders Germany. The discipline of the Roman soldiers triumphed, and by day's end most of the German army was destroyed. Ariovistus barely escaped and died soon after.

Caesar planned to occupy the Rhine frontier and prevent more German migration. In northern Gaul (modern Belgium) the powerful Belgae confederacy defied the Romans. All winter long, both sides prepared for war. One of the tribes pretended to surrender to Caesar, but it was a trick. They suddenly attacked. Caesar defeated them and sold the 53,000 survivors into slavery. This stopped the resistance, at least for a while.

THE STRUGGLE FOR POWER

When news of Caesar's victories reached Rome, the Senate arranged for a fifteen-day public thanksgiving. Caesar was now as powerful as Pompey. Like Pompey, he had an army that was loyal to him directly. Pompey was becoming jealous, so he began to en-

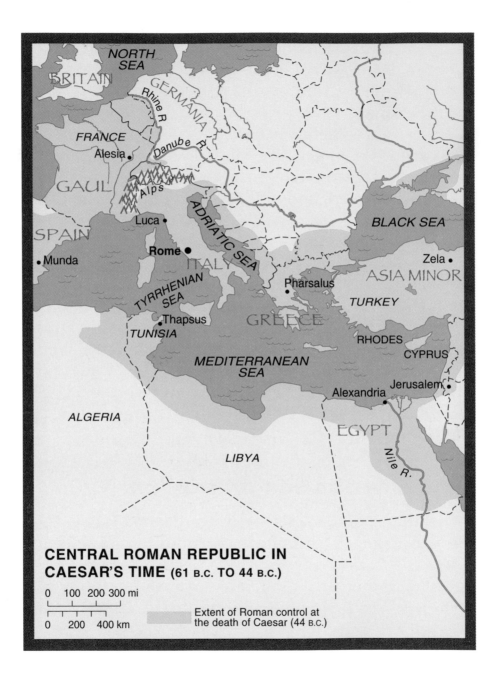

NORTH SEA

BRITAIN

GERMANIA

Rhine R.

FRANCE

Alesia •

Danube R.

GAUL

Alps

SPAIN

Luca •

BLACK SEA

ADRIATIC SEA

Munda •

Rome •

ITALY

Zela •

ASIA MINOR

Pharsalus •

TURKEY

TYRRHENIAN SEA

GREECE

• Thapsus

TUNISIA

RHODES

CYPRUS

MEDITERRANEAN SEA

ALGERIA

Alexandria •

Jerusalem •

EGYPT

LIBYA

Nile R.

CENTRAL ROMAN REPUBLIC IN
CAESAR'S TIME (61 B.C. TO 44 B.C.)

0 100 200 300 mi

0 200 400 km

Extent of Roman control at
the death of Caesar (44 B.C.)

courage Caesar's enemies, including Cicero, to oppose the Triumvirate. Caesar became worried and asked Pompey and Crassus to meet with him again. The three met in April of 56 B.C. in the Cisalpine village of Luca.

At Luca, the men arranged for Pompey and Crassus to be consuls for the year 55. After their year in office, Pompey was appointed proconsul of Spain and Crassus proconsul of Syria. Caesar's governorship of Gaul was extended for five years.

When Caesar left Luca, a massive revolt was underway in Gaul. He personally led a fleet of new, light galleys (warships propelled by rowing) along the west coast of Gaul to fight the seafaring Veneti tribe. Caesar brutally executed their captured chiefs and sold the others into slavery.

In the spring two more Germanic tribes crossed into Gaul. After a brief clash with the Romans, their leaders came to Caesar to negotiate a peace. Caesar arrested them and marched his troops after their people. He meant this as a warning to all the tribes. He ruthlessly slaughtered the Germanic warriors along with their women and children as they tried to escape across the Rhine River to safety in Germany.

In Rome, Cicero and Cato, defenders of the traditional Republic, denounced Caesar's cruelty against the Germans. But it did not matter what the senators

*This model
depicts the series of obstacles
that Caesar used at the siege at Alesia. The
Romans used these siegeworks to hold the Gallic army in
their hill fortress while fending off other Gallic troops who
attempted to relieve the siege. The battle of Alesia showed
Caesar to be, like his hero Alexander the Great, a master of
military strategy.*

said. The three men of the Triumvirate had become
too powerful to be bothered by the complaints of
unarmed senators and speechmakers. Caesar moved
on toward a new conquest—Britain.

EXPANDING ROME'S INFLUENCE

The British Isles had long fascinated the Romans. In their minds it was a land of mythology dangerously near the end of the world. In 55 B.C. Caesar crossed the English Channel. For eighteen days he fought with the island tribesmen. The Britons fought with chariots and long spears, and they struck much fear into the small Roman raiding party. After this fighting, Caesar was forced to quit the island, but in the spring of 54 B.C. he returned with more troops. He forced the British tribal leaders to surrender.

Caesar found it easier to win a quick victory, however, than to install a permanent Roman government in Britain. Britain would one day come under Roman control, but not in Caesar's time. Meanwhile, the situation in Gaul became alarming.

In the autumn of 54 B.C., Caesar crossed back into Gaul and discovered that the Gauls had revolted. They had slaughtered some Roman forces and were holding others under siege. Romans usually did not wage war in the winter, but Caesar was determined to smother the revolt before it flamed into an uncontrollable blaze.

He marched his troops through the frigid and snowy Gallic frontier with remarkable speed. At first he crushed the Gallic tribes. But a young chief named Vercingetorix believed that the Romans could be

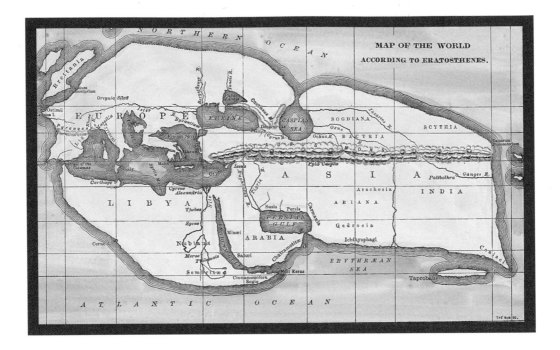

This map shows the Roman conception of the world. The term "Asia" was used to describe the area from the Middle East all the way to India. The term "Libya" described all of North Africa, including Egypt. The island in the upper left corner of the map labeled "Brettania" represents Great Britain.

defeated. He united the tribes of Gaul into a single army. By 53 B.C. it appeared that Caesar's work had been undone: all of Gaul was armed and calling for the destruction of the Roman invaders.

Perhaps for the first time in his life Caesar faced a

Julius Caesar often led his troops into battle in person. His presence on the battlefield inspired courage in his men. Here Caesar urges the Roman legions forward against the wild-looking natives of Britain.

Caesar receives the surrender of the Gallic chieftain Vercingetorix with cold satisfaction. Caesar treated his enemies ruthlessly until they submitted to his will.

brave and skillful general, equipped with a vast army and all the supplies of Gaul. In 52 B.C., on the plateau of Alesia (near modern Dijon, France), Caesar finally laid siege to the Gallic army, which was waiting in a hilltop fortress.

The Roman soldiers went to work with shovels and set in ten miles of fortifications around the Gallic stronghold. They built three outer circles of defense to protect themselves against sudden attacks from Gauls trying to protect Vercingetorix. More than forty Gallic tribes marched on Caesar's outer defenses, and Vercingetorix sent his forces down on the Romans at the same time. Caesar personally led the Roman cavalry into battle, and the Romans fended off the double-sided attack.

After a month of fighting and bloodshed, Vercingetorix threw down his weapons and surrendered to Caesar. The vast army of Vercingetorix, wrote the Greek historian Plutarch, vanished "like a ghost or a dream." Gaul had come securely under the control of Rome.

4

THE CIVIL WAR

Caesar wrote a history of the Gallic Wars that was distributed immediately in Rome. He had to reenter Roman politics, and his writings were a perfect way to advertise his greatness. After his exploits in Gaul he had more fame, wealth, and military power than anyone in Rome. Many feared that he would seize control of the government.

The optimates in the Senate had, in fact, made an uneasy peace with Pompey. Pompey had raised troops for the Spanish province but had never departed. Instead, he was trying to gain support from Caesar's enemies in Rome. Many senators saw Caesar as the greatest threat to the Roman Republic. They thought Pompey was the lesser of two evils.

This arch in Orange, France, was built by Caesar's adopted son, the Emperor Augustus Caesar, to commemorate Caesar's victory over the Gauls.

The Triumvirate became weak while Caesar was in Gaul and fell apart completely when Crassus lost a battle against the Parthians. Supposedly Crassus's head was delivered to the Parthian king on a platter. The king poured molten gold down Crassus's throat and said, "Here, you have been greedy for this all your life. Eat it now."

FROM ALLIES TO ENEMIES

Without Crassus, the alliance between Pompey and Caesar crumbled. It got worse when Julia, the daughter of Caesar and wife of Pompey, died in 54 B.C. The two men grew apart, and each one wanted to be the greatest leader of Rome.

Instead of governing Spain, Pompey was working to gain the support of the Romans and turn them against Caesar. Caesar made several attempts to pacify Pompey and avoid a war. He offered to disband his armies and return to Rome as a private citizen if Pompey would do the same. But leading senators threatened to prosecute Caesar in the law courts for corruption and bribery if he tried to return to Rome.

Late in the year 50 B.C. Caesar and Pompey drew up their armies. Pompey was encamped in Italy. Caesar had recently marched from Gaul toward Italy and encamped along a small river called the Rubicon. The Rubicon divided the Roman province of Cisalpine Gaul from Italy itself.

On January 10, 49 B.C., Caesar set free some horses to please the gods, then crossed the Rubicon. By entering into his Italian homeland without disbanding his armies, Caesar had become an outlaw of the

Roman Republic. When he crossed the Rubicon he declared, "The die is cast," meaning there was no turning back.

Remembering how Caesar had slaughtered the Gauls and the Germans, the citizens of Rome panicked. The city was engulfed in confusion and disor-

This French magazine advertisement (for canned meat) shows Caesar fording the Rubicon. The quotation at the bottom reads: "'The die is cast!' cries Julius Caesar, then consul, and he crosses the Rubicon with his army, in spite of the prohibition of the Senate, thus unveiling his scheme to become dictator."

der. Many senators had feared the rise of a tyrant, a single man who would replace their authority. Now they were forced to choose between two such men, Caesar and Pompey. Pompey's supporters moved to the east coast of Italy, and Pompey was preparing to sail across the Adriatic Sea to Greece to gather his army for battle. Caesar's supporters hurried north.

Pompey still had a vast army in Spain. Caesar realized that he could not leave such a danger at his back while he pursued Pompey to Greece. He said, "I am going to Spain to fight an army without a general, and then to the east to fight a general without an army."

Caesar laid siege to Pompey's army in Spain and defeated them without much trouble. He was very careful about spilling Roman blood, for these soldiers were his countrymen. He knew that he must win the support of the people in order to restore order in Rome. He went back to Rome and was appointed temporary dictator; this meant he could officially use the treasury to pay for his war against Pompey.

POMPEY STRIKES BACK

Caesar could not linger in Rome, because Pompey's army was growing. In 48 B.C. Caesar sailed for Greece. He had referred to Pompey as a general without an army. But in fact Pompey had more troops than Caesar. Also, they were well supplied, while Caesar's troops had little food and were worn out from the Spanish expedition.

The war did not look very promising for Caesar. He was fighting Romans, after all, who were professional soldiers, unlike the tribesmen of Gaul. The two commanders also fought with similar tactics and weapons. But Caesar commanded a stronger allegiance from his troops. His soldiers would endure any hardship.

After nine months of maneuvering and siege, both armies were desperately short of supplies. Finally, Pompey was goaded into battle by his eager generals. The Battle of Pharsalus was fought on August 9, 48 B.C., in Greece. The heat and dust were unbearable, and Caesar was outnumbered. But Caesar's strategy scattered Pompey's cavalry charge, and he drove his own troops forward.

Caesar shouted, "Spare your fellow citizens!" But his men slaughtered fifteen thousand of Pompey's soldiers. Caesar's army suffered far fewer losses. Pompey's will broke as he saw his army being cut down, and he fled from the battlefield. The last of Pompey's legions had little choice but to surrender. And Caesar was elected dictator.

At the Battle of Pharsalus, Caesar made it clear that Pompey's days of greatness were over. Pompey's panicked flight from the battle, shown here, meant Caesar had won the Civil War.

5

ETERNAL DICTATOR

After the Battle of Pharsalus, Pompey fled east to Asia Minor. Eventually he went to Egypt. He had once donated soldiers and gold to help Egypt's ruler, Ptolemy XII. So this was the place for Pompey to find help and raise an army large enough to defeat Caesar.

Caesar arrived in Egypt just a few days after Pompey. When he landed, he was presented with Pompey's head. Egypt was in a state of anarchy. Ptolemy XII had died, leaving his four children to fight each other for the throne. The ten-year-old Ptolemy XIII was ruling Egypt with the help of a power-hungry adviser named Pothinus. They were the ones who killed Pompey, hoping to gain Caesar's favor.

*Caesar was moved to tears when he was
presented with the head of Pompey the Great.
Although they were enemies in the Civil War,
Caesar had admired Pompey.*

Caesar is said to have wept at the sight of Pompey's head. Pompey had once been the greatest man in Rome, and now his head rotted in the relentless Egyptian sun. Caesar decided to stay in the capital, Alexandria, but when the Romans marched into the city the Egyptians attacked them. The Egyptians thought the Romans had come as conquerors. Caesar found himself almost a prisoner in the palace at Alexandria with his small number of troops.

CAESAR MEETS CLEOPATRA

Cleopatra, the twenty-year-old sister of Ptolemy XIII, wanted to challenge her brother and seize the throne for herself. She decided to appeal to Caesar for help. She had her servant wrap her inside a carpet and carry the package directly past the palace guards to Caesar. When the rug was presented as a gift to Caesar, Cleopatra leaped out.

The trick impressed Caesar. In fact, he fell in love with her and decided to help her obtain power in Egypt. When Caesar chose her side, the people of Alexandria revolted. Caesar attempted to protect his troops from a siege in the palace by sending small war parties into the city. He then quickly sent for reinforcements from the Roman province of Syria. When the Roman troops arrived, they fought the main battle of what Caesar called the Alexandrine War. Ptolemy XIII was killed in this battle. Caesar placed Cleopatra on the throne of Egypt. Then he enjoyed a luxurious cruise down the Nile River with her to celebrate their victory and to see the wondrous sights of Egypt.

After months of feasting and celebrations with Cleopatra, Caesar left Egypt. He had other Roman provinces to conquer. Near Zela in Asia Minor he defeated Pharnaces II, the son of Rome's old enemy Mithradates. After the brief battle, Caesar summed up the campaign in a dispatch to Rome with the famous words *veni, vidi, vici* ("I came, I saw, I conquered").

Caesar wanted to destroy Pompey's sons, too. They had raised an army in North Africa with the help of Cato, an old enemy of Caesar and a defender of the traditional Roman Republic. They also had the help of Numidian cavalrymen, who were fierce fighters on horseback. Caesar invaded North Africa at the end of

This mosaic shows Roman troops on the shore of the Nile River. Caesar found himself desperately short of soldiers during the Alexandrine War and had to send to Syria for reinforcements. Soldiers from Greece and the Middle East fought for both sides during this war.

47 B.C. He finally overpowered the rebels at the city of Thapsus (in modern Tunisia) in April of 46.

ENJOYING VICTORY

In July Caesar returned to Rome, was made dictator for ten years, and celebrated his victories. A Roman general could be given an official celebration, called a triumph, for a very successful campaign. Caesar celebrated four triumphs for his victories in Gaul, Egypt, Asia Minor, and North Africa. No other Roman ever received so many.

Caesar also staged fantastic exhibitions. Sea fights were conducted on a vast artificial lake that turned crimson as the bloodied victims plunged into its waters. Land battles complete with elephants were staged, and prisoners, including the Gaul Vercingetorix, were paraded through the streets of Rome before being executed.

Meanwhile, Pompey's two sons went to Spain and assembled a powerful army. The threat became so serious that Caesar led his own army to Spain in November of 46 B.C. He defeated the brothers at Munda in March of 45. Caesar celebrated a triumph for his victory, but this one offended many Romans. Triumphs were for victories over foreign enemies. It was not proper to celebrate the deaths of fellow Romans in civil conflict.

MAJOR OFFICES
HELD BY JULIUS CAESAR

Priest of Jupiter (87 B.C.): Jupiter was principal god of the Romans. The priesthood of Jupiter was drawn primarily from the young sons of senatorial families.

Quaestor (68 B.C.): manager of the finances of Rome or of a province. Obtaining this seat automatically insured the holder a seat in the Roman Senate.

Curule Aedile (65 B.C.): a magistrate responsible for maintenance of Rome itself, such as corn supplies, streets, markets, water supply, and public buildings. The curule aedile also oversaw the Roman Games, a duty that could bring him much public recognition and entry into political circles.

Pontifex Maximus (63 B.C.): the chief official of the Order of Pontiffs, which presided over national religion. The office was won by election.

Praetor (62 B.C.): judge next in seniority to consul. Praetors tried cases in the law courts.

Triumvir: one of the three members of the First Triumvirate formed by Caesar, Pompey, and Crassus in 60 B.C. The Triumvirate was unofficial, and the triumvirs were not recognized by the Roman government.

Consul (59 B.C.): the highest civil and military office in Rome. Two consuls were elected at a time and divided power between themselves for one year.

Dictator (48, 47, 45 B.C.): an independent leader of the Roman State in times of civil or military crisis. Originally a dictator was required by law to step down after six months, but Caesar was made dictator for six months, two years, and then for life.

Cleopatra arrived in Rome to celebrate with Caesar, but her presence there also offended many. She brought her son Caesarion, who, she claimed, was the son of Caesar. Caesar refused to acknowledge Caesarion as his son, but he treated Cleopatra as an honored guest. When he unveiled a golden statue of Cleopatra in Rome, some people thought he would marry her and rule Rome from Alexandria.

Caesar had no such plans, but rumors of plots and conspiracies against him were whispered throughout Rome. He had been voted dictator for life in 45 B.C. To many people, that meant the Republic was dead. He showed no sign that he would ever restore the full powers of the Roman Senate.

Caesar used his powers justly, giving Rome many needed reforms. He ordered the construction of splendid public works around the city. He distributed land to his many followers. He increased the grain

Caesar rides through Rome in a Triumph to celebrate his various victories. With him is his son by Cleopatra, Caesarion. The standard behind his chariot reads S. P. Q. R., which stands for the Latin Senatus Populusque Romanus—*the Senate and Roman People. On top is the imperial eagle, a symbol feared by the enemies of Rome.*

ration to the poor. He even adjusted the Roman calendar (the month of July is named for him); the old calendar did not match the actual seasons and made it hard to schedule festivals, elections, and even seed planting.

Despite Caesar's reforms, many Romans still resented being ruled by a single man. Not since the early days of Rome had one man ruled independently for such a long time. A dictator was supposed to be for emergencies, and then only for six months, not for life. Some who were worried, like Brutus, were Caesar's friends, but they decided that only by killing him could they save the Republic. That is why they plunged their daggers into Caesar's body in 44 B.C.

CAESAR'S LEGACY

Julius Caesar was a man of action. Through sheer willpower he marked Rome with his personality, and his influence was felt throughout the ancient world for centuries after his death. He was also a man of many talents. He was highly educated and would have been famous for his writings alone—the histories, which have survived, and his poetry, which is lost. He loved to discuss the writings and ideas of ancient authors. All in all, he was an extraordinary citizen of Rome.

Soon after Caesar was killed, though, the Roman

Republic also died. Caesar's adopted son, Octavius, and his lieutenant, Marc Antony, defeated his chief assassins in 42 B.C. Then they turned on each other. The civil war between Octavius and Antony finally killed the Republic. Octavius prevailed and took the position that Caesar would not—first emperor of Rome. Like all the Roman emperors to come after him, Octavius adopted the name Caesar.

Even after the last Caesar ruled Rome, despots and kings used the name Caesar to invoke the powers of supreme command—in Russian, *czar* (or *tsar*); in German, *kaiser*; and in Arabic, *qaysar*. Perhaps because of his absolute power, Julius Caesar will live always as the symbol of the eternal tyrant.

TIMELINE

100 B.C.	Gaius Julius Caesar born
87 B.C.	Caesar appointed priest of Jupiter
84 B.C.	Caesar marries Cornelia
c. 76 B.C.	Birth of Julia to Caesar and Cornelia
75 B.C.	Caesar kidnapped by pirates in Mediterranean; after he is freed he captures and crucifies the pirates
69 B.C.	Caesar appointed as governor of Farther Spain
67 B.C.	Caesar marries Pompeia
65–62 B.C.	Caesar serves as curule aedile, pontifex maximus, and praetor in Rome
61–60 B.C.	Caesar serves as governor of Farther Spain
60 B.C.	First Triumvirate formed by Caesar, Pompey, and Crassus
59 B.C.	Caesar chosen as consul; marries Calpurnia
58–51 B.C.	Gallic Wars
55 B.C.	Caesar invades Britain
52 B.C.	Caesar defeats Vercingetorix at Alesia, bringing Gaul under Roman control
49 B.C.	Caesar crosses the Rubicon, effectively starting Civil War
48 B.C.	Caesar defeats Pompey at Pharsalus, arrives in Egypt, meets Cleopatra; Caesar's Alexandrine War
47 B.C.	Caesar invades North Africa; Caesarion born
46 B.C.	Four Triumphs for Caesar's victories in Gaul, Egypt, Asia Minor, and North Africa held in Rome
45 B.C.	Caesar defeats Pompey's sons at Munda in Spain, is voted dictator for life
March 15, 44 B.C.	The Ides of March—Caesar assassinated at a meeting of the Senate

FOR MORE INFORMATION

FOR FURTHER READING

Dupuy, Trevor Nevitt. *The Military Life of Julius Caesar: Imperator*. New York: Franklin Watts, 1969.

Fry, Plantagenet Somerset. *Great Caesar*. London: William Collins & Sons, 1974.

Komroff, Manuel. *Julius Caesar*. New York: Julian Messner, Inc., 1955.

FOR ADVANCED READERS

Fuller, J. F. *Julius Caesar: Man, Soldier, and Tyrant*. New York: Da Capo, 1991.

Grant, Michael. *Julius Caesar*. New York: M. Evans & Co., 1992.

Plutarch. *The Lives of the Noble Grecians and Romans*. Translated by Sir Thomas North. London: Oxford University Press, 1927.

Taylor, Lily R. *Party Politics in the Age of Caesar*. Berkeley: University of California Press, 1949.

WORKS BY JULIUS CAESAR

The Civil War. Translated by Jane F. Gardner. New York: Dorset Press, 1976.

The Gallic Wars. Translated by John Warrington. New York: The Heritage Press, 1955.

FAMOUS RETELLINGS OF CAESAR'S LIFE

Shakespeare, William. *Julius Caesar*. Joseph L. Mankiewicz directed a classic movie version of this play in 1953. It starred John Gielgud, Marlon Brando, James Mason, Edmond O'Brien, Greer Garson, and Deborah Kerr.

Shaw, George Bernard. *Caesar and Cleopatra*. This also was made into a movie, directed by Gabriel Pascal and starring Claude Rains and Vivien Leigh.

INTERNET SITES

Home pages and directories will link you to a myriad of Web sites about the ancient Mediterranean world:

Exploring Ancient World Cultures (University of Evansville):
http://cedar.evansville.edu/~wcweb/wc101/

ArchNet (University of Connecticut):
http://spirit.lib.uconn.edu/archaeology.html

ROMARCH, a home page on archaeology in Italy and the Roman provinces:
http://personal-www.umich.edu/~pfoss/ROMARCH.html

The Ancient World Web:
http://atlantic.evsc.virginia.edu/julia/AncientWorld.html

INDEX

Page numbers in *italics* refer to illustrations

ABOUT THE AUTHOR

Robert Green is a freelance writer who lives in New York City. He holds a B.A. in English literature from Boston University and is the author of *"Vive la France": The French Resistance during World War II*. He has also written biographies of five other important figures of the ancient world: *Alexander the Great, Cleopatra, Hannibal, Herod the Great,* and *Tutankhamun.*